The AVIV Haggadah

© 2021 Chryl Elizabeth McWilliams & Barry Page
St. Clair Publications

All rights reserved. No part of this publication may be reproduced or transmitted in any form by any means electronic or mechanical, including telecopy, recording, or any information storage and retrieval system now known or invented, without permission in writing from the publisher, except by a reviewer who wishes to quote brief passages in connection with a review written for inclusion in a magazine, newspaper or broadcast.

ISBN 978-1-947514-42-3

Printed in the United States of America

St. Clair Publications P. O. Box 726 Mc Minnville, TN 37111—0726

http://stclairpublications.com

Cover Design

Kent Grey-Hesselbein Design Studio
www.kghdesignstudio.com

The AVIV Haggadah

Chryl Elizabeth McWilliams

Barry Page

Songs are traditional

THE FESTIVAL OF AVIV HAGGADAH

We open our service with the Shema:

Listen Israel YHVH our God YHVH is ONE
You shall love God exceedingly: with all your heart and all your being

Because it is such a special occasion we continue with the Shachahanu:
Blessed are you YHVH our God, king of the universe, that allowed us to live
Be established and to arrive to this special occasion

The sun has been shining the birds are still chirping
All nature is blooming in its springtime best
In ancient Israel it was the time of the barley harvest AVIV
It was the time of the year of the liberation of the nation Israel
From the Egyptian slavery and into a world of freedom and love.

Let us enjoy the beauty of our world and all its living beings HALLELU YAH
Thanking our creator for the freedom that we have at hand HALLELU YAH
Thanking YAH for the harvests that this earth yields HALLELU YAH
And for the enjoyment we can have on this festival HALLELU YAH

The Three Harvest Festivals

Moses before his death conceived of three national harvest pilgrimages in Israel:
Firstly, Aviv at the start of the barley harvest,
Then Shavuot, seven weeks later, at the start of the wheat harvest;
Finally, Sukkot at the height of the wheat and grape harvest.

In Deuteronomy 16 the three harvests were promulgated;

The AVIV Haggadah

Observe the month of Aviv-the barley harvest, and keep a pilgrimage festival to YHVH your God; for in the month of Aviv YHVH your God brought you out of Egypt by night. You shall bring to YHVH your God, the first barley sheaves of your harvest and of your flock and herd, to the place where YHVH shall choose to cause His name to dwell there. You shalt cook and eat the meat of your cows and sheep in the chosen place; You shall rejoice before YHVH your God, you and your children, your servants, the Levites that are in your gates, the stranger, the fatherless and the widow, and you shall turn in the morning, and return to your tents. You shall remember that YHVH took you out of Egypt in the month of the barley harvest-Aviv.

Seven weeks shall you number; from the time the sickle is first put to the standing wheat. You shalt keep the feast of weeks to YHVH your God after the measure of the freewill which you give, according as YHVH your God has blessed you. You shall rejoice before YHVH your God, you, and your sons, and your daughters, your man-servant, and maid-servant, and the Levite that is in your gates, and the stranger, and the fatherless, and the widow, that are in the midst of you, in the place which YHVH your God shall choose to cause His name to dwell there. You shall remember that you were a bondman in Egypt; you shall observe and do these statutes.

You shall keep the feast of tabernacles seven days, after you have harvested from your threshing-floor and from your winepress. You shall rejoice in the feast, you, and your sons and daughters, and your man-servant, and maid-servant, and the Levite, and the stranger, and the fatherless, and the widow, that are within thy gates. Seven days shalt you keep this feast to YHVH your God in the place which YHVH shall choose; because YHVH your God shall bless you in all your increase, and in all the work of your hands, and you shall be altogether joyful.

Three times in a year shall all shall appear before YHVH your God in the place which He shall choose; on the feast of Aviv, and on the feast of weeks, and on the feast of tabernacles; and they shall not appear before YHVH empty; every man shall give as he is able, according to the blessing of YHVH your God which He has given you. Deut 16:1-17

The code of Deuteronomy [chapters 1-30] is generally free of animal sacrificial references and the Moses Scroll is completely free of any sacrificial material. Moses was a pure monotheist who did not associate with altars- tables where animals were killed and cooked to feed hungry semi-gods. All the Torah prophets, who followed Moses approach, utterly rejected animal sacrifice on numerous occasions. The first pilgrimage festival text in chapter 16 of Deuteronomy has clearly been added to with sacrificial material that has been deleted in the quote above.

The original Festival of AVIV, as presented by Moses, can be seen as a harvest pilgrimage where all Israel would travel and meet at a proposed capitol city carrying the first sheaves of the barley harvest, offering tithes to the Levites and the needy, and celebrating the anniversary of the Exodus from Egypt. The actual word AVIV can be translated as "ripe barley grains."

For the feast of Sukkot see page 21.

When the pilgrim brought the sheaves to the Levites he would say:

"My father was a wandering Aramean, and he went down into Egypt with a few people and lived there and became a great nation, powerful and numerous. But the Egyptians mistreated them and made them suffer, subjecting them to harsh labor. Then we cried out to YHVH, the God of our ancestors, and YHVH heard our voice and saw our misery, toil and oppression. So YHVH brought us out of Egypt with a mighty hand and an outstretched arm, with great terror and with signs and wonders. He brought us to this place and gave us this land, a land flowing with milk and honey; and now I bring the firstfruits of the soil that you, YHVH, have given me."

Then place the basket before YHVH your God and bow down before him. Deut 26: 4-20

There was also a triannual tithe.

At the end of every three years, bring all the tithes of that year's produce and store it in your towns, so that the Levites (who have no allotment or inheritance of their own) and the foreigners, the fatherless and the widows who live in your towns may come and eat and be satisfied, and so that YHVH your God may bless you in all the work of your hands. Deut. 14:28-29

Our first song tonight Shibolet Basadeh is a modern Israeli song expressing the joy of the barley harvest:

SHIBOLET BASADEH
Hebrew and Translation

Shibolet Bashadah kor'ah baru'ach	Ear of grain in the field, bowed in the wind
Me'omes gar'inim ki rav.	From the weight of its seed which is great.
Uvemerchav harim	And in the expanse of the mountains
Yom kavar yafu'ach.	The day already rises.
Hashemech ketem v'zahav.	The sun is fine gold.
Uhu ho uro	Arise, oh arise,
Shuru beni kfarim	Look, sons of the village.
Kama hen basha kvar	The tall grain has already ripened
Al pnei hakarim.	in the meadows
Kitzru, shilchu magal	Harvest, extend the scythe -
Et reshit hakatzir.	It's time for the beginning of the harvest
Sdei se'orim tama	A pure field of barley
Zer chang oreret	Is crowned with a holiday wreath.
Shefa y'vul uvracha.	An abundance of produce and blessing.
Likrat bo hakotzrim	Just before the coming of the harvesters,
B'zohar mozheret	With shining brilliance,
Cheresh la'omer m'chaka.	Silently, it waits for the sheaf.
Havu, hanafu,	Come, brandish (the scythe)
Niru lachem nir.	Plow for yourselves the broken-up field.
Chag la cama	It's a holiday for the standing grain,
Et reshit katzir.	The time of the beginning of the harvest.
Kitzru, shilchu magal	Harvest extend the scythe -
Et reshit hakatzir.	It's time for the beginning of the harvest.

Moses in his writings talked of Israel as "a land flowing with milk and honey" and we will now sing:

ERETZ ZEVAT HALAV UDEVASH

Eretz Zevat Halav ve Devash   A Land Flowing with Milk and Honey

The path from the slavery of Israel in Egypt to the settling in a land flowing with milk and honey was an incredible one filled with signs and wonders - natural events that Israel attributed to the one God YHVH that lovingly liberated the founding nation of Israel.

Head of Moses, Michelangelo

We are first focusing on Mount Thera, an enormous volcano on a Grecian island that erupted at around 1500 BCE that is 3500 years ago. The Canadian/ Israeli archaeologist Simcha Jaacovici is one of many scholars who links the Exodus of Israel with the eruption of Thera and his video "The Exodus Decoded" presents in detail the reasons why the Exodus should be seen as a response to the Mount Thera eruption.

Ask now about the former days, long before your time, from the day God created human beings on the earth; ask from one end of the heavens to the other. Has anything so great as this ever happened, or has anything like it ever been heard of? Has any other people heard the voice of God speaking out of fire, as you have, and lived? Has any god ever tried to take for himself one nation out of another nation, by testings, by signs and wonders, by war, by a mighty hand and an outstretched arm, or by great and awesome deeds, like all the things YHVH your God did for you in Egypt before your very eyes.

Deut. 4:33-34

We have arrived at Thera a Grecian island, today call Santorini. There was an immense volcano that erupted there 3500-3600 years ago. It was one of the largest eruptions witnessed by mankind. Aktori was a city near the volcano and it experienced an explosion equivalent to 40 atomic bombs. No human remains were found as they were covered by an immense ash layer. Possibly as many as 20,000 people were killed as a result of the volcano. Most of the Minoan civilisation, at that time, were killed or fled from the area.

A volcano like Mount Thera

The Egyptians also suffered the consequences of the outpourings of Thera, that disrupted Pharaoh's control over Egypt, including its slave population. Moses, the spiritual leader of Israel at this time, at the command of the one God of Israel, liberated the monotheistic nation out of the land of Egypt and ended the oppressive slavery. The mixed nation, led by the Levites and the sons of Jacob, planned to travel back to Canaan, the original home of Jacob and his sons.

Sing **BETZET YISRAEL MIMITTZRAIM**

Betzet Yisrael memitzrayim
Bet Yaakov meumloez
Hayetah Yehudah lekodsho
Yisrael Mumshelootav.

Hayam raah veyanos
Hayarden yisov leahor
Heharim rukde keelim
Gevaot kivne tzon.

Malecha Hayam Kitanoos
Hayarden Tisov leahor
Milfne adon huli aretz
Milfne aloha yaakov

Hahofhi hatzur agam mayim
Halmish le maano mayim.

1 When Israel came out of Egypt,
Jacob from a people of foreign tongue,

2 Judah became God's sanctuary,
Israel his dominion.

3 The sea looked and fled,
the Jordan turned back;

4 the mountains leaped like rams,
the hills like lambs.

5 Why was it, sea, that you fled?
Why, Jordan, did you turn back?

6 Why, mountains, did you leap like rams,
you hills, like lambs?

7 Tremble, earth,
at the presence of the Lord,
at the presence of the God of Jacob,

8 who turned the rock into a pool,
the hard rock into springs of water.

The Israelites came to a place called PIHAHIROT on the YAM SUF, the Sea of Reeds, just to the east of the Nile Delta. The new nation of Israel then started inland into the Sinai Peninsula. Meanwhile Pharaoh organized his army and chariots with the aim of returning the fleeing slaves to their servitude. The chariots reached PIHAHIROT with the intention of travelling west on the coastal road, this being the shortest way for the slaves to reach Canaan. A powerful Tsunami, caused by the Thera eruption drowned and killed Pharaoh's soldiers who were travelling on the sea road. The liberation of the monotheistic community, led by Moses, was now complete.

A tsunami like that which drowned the Egyptian chariots on the shore of the Sea of Reeds

The AVIV Haggadah

For generations, even thousands of years the Israelite nation sang.

Sing **AVADIM HAYINU**:

Avadim Hayinu	**We Were Slaves**
Avadim hayinu, hayinu	We were slaves, we were slaves,
Ata bene horin	We were slaves, we were slaves,
Bene horin	Now we're free, we're free.
Avadim hayinu	We were slaves,
Ata bene horin	Now, we're free.
Avadim hayinu	We were slaves
Ata ata bene horin	Now we're free, we're free.
Bene horin	Now we're free, we're free.

Slaves in Egypt

The events leading up to the liberation of Israel from Egypt were natural- related to a volcano however to the people of Israel and their prophet Moses this was clearly the one God YHVH acting through nature in a glorious act of liberation of a nation that had faith in the one God, YHVH. There was one more event that made this conclusion absolutely clear.

Mount Horeb/Sinai

After crossing the Sinai Peninsula, the nation of Israel [struggler for God] reached a place called by Moses, Horeb [wilderness]. Here, a clearly incredible event occurred. In both the Code of Deuteronomy and the Moses scroll it is told that the one God spoke in a human voice some, or all, of the Ten Words to the congregation of Israel based at the foot of a mountain in Horeb. God even inscribed tablets of stone with the text of the Ten Words. We have no idea how this happened.

When God speaks we are speechless.

It appeared that God wanted to make it clear that the one God was behind the apparently natural liberation of the nation Israel "I am YHVH your God who brought you out of the land of bondage" and express the moral standards ZEDEK that were expected of the newly formed nation in their travels.

Before Moses died on Mount Nebo he looked out over the land of Israel. This is the view that we see from Mount Nebo today.

THE MOSES SCROLL VERSION OF THE TEN WORDS

The Covenant of Love

The Ten Words revelation at Horeb was an introduction by YHVH to the people of Israel. Around forty years later before the death of Moses a covenant of love was made between God and Israel that was based on the exceeding, loyal love by Israel for God "with all your heart and all your being."{Deut. 6]

At the time of the forefathers there was love between Abraham, Isaac and Jacob and the one God.{Deut 10:15] With the covenant of Nebo this love was expected to be between a nation Israel and God when Israel was settled in their new homeland. This was the climax of the national, spiritual life of Moses and would hopefully set the stage for the future religious life of the nation Israel.

Before his death, Moses wrote the Moses Scroll which was a combination of the Ten Words and the Covenant of Love. The Scroll ends with the confirmation of a blessing and curse.

Joshua crossing the Jordan

Joshua, Mount Gerizim and Mount Eval

Before his death Moses also commanded his successor Joshua to arrange a ceremony to be conducted at the two mountains Gerizim and Eval that were situated near Gilgal on the west side of the Jordan river. At the ceremony the Levites would read out the Torah of Moses and the people Israel would stand on the two mountains either side of the Levites and respond to the blessing and curse by saying Amen. This Joshua did [Moses Scroll GC7-HB3]

Mount Gerizim and Mount Eval

Joshua also conducted a Covenant Renewed at Shechem

The closing speech of Joshua is recorded in Joshua chapters 24/25. We will close our AVIV celebration with the reading of Joshua's speech:

Then Joshua assembled all the tribes of Israel at Shechem. He summoned the elders, leaders, judges and officials of Israel, and they presented themselves before God.

Joshua said to all the people, "This is what YHVH, the God of Israel, says: 'Long ago your ancestors, including Terah the father of Abraham and Nahor, lived beyond the [Jordan] River and worshiped other gods. But I took your father Abraham from the land beyond the [Jordan] River and led him throughout Canaan and gave him many descendants. I gave him Isaac, and to Isaac I gave Jacob and Esau. I assigned the hill country of Seir to Esau, but Jacob and his family went down to Egypt.

'Then I sent Moses and Aaron, and I afflicted the Egyptians by what I did there, and I brought you out. When I brought your people out of Egypt, you came to the sea, and the Egyptians pursued with chariots and horsemen as far as the Reed Sea. You cried to YHVH for help, and he put darkness between you and the Egyptians; he brought the sea over them and covered them. You saw with your own eyes what I did to the Egyptians. Then you lived in the wilderness for a long time.

'I brought you to the land of the Amorites who lived east of the Jordan. They fought against you, but I gave them into your hands. I destroyed them from before you, and you took possession of their land. When Balak son of Zippor, the king of Moab, prepared to fight against Israel, he sent for Balaam son of Peor to put a curse on you. But I would not listen to Balaam, so he blessed you again and again, and I delivered you out of his hand.

'You crossed the Jordan and you came to Jericho and fought against them [the people of Jericho] and did to them as you did to the Amorites, Perizzites, Canaanites, Hittites, Girgashites, Hivites and Jebusites, and I gave them into your hands. I sent the hornet ahead of you, which drove them out before you—also the two Amorite kings. You did not do it [alone] with your own sword and bow. It was God who gave you the land for which you did not toil and cities you did not build; and you live in them and eat from vineyards and olive groves that you did not plant.'

"Now fear YHVH and serve him with humility. Throw away the gods your ancestors worshipped beyond the River and in Egypt, and serve YHVH. If, however, serving YHVH seems undesirable to you, then choose for yourselves this day whom you will serve, whether the gods your ancestors served beyond the River, or the gods of the Amorites, in whose land you are living. But as for me and my household, we will serve YHVH."

Then the people answered, "Far be it from us to forsake YHVH to serve other gods! It was YHVH our God himself who brought us and our parents up out of Egypt, from that land of slavery, and performed those great signs before our eyes. He protected us on our entire journey and among all the nations through which we traveled. The Lord drove out before us all the nations, including the Amorites, who lived in the land. We too will serve YHVH, because he is our God."

Joshua said to the people, "You are not able to serve YHVH. He is a holy God; he is a zealous God. He will not forgive your rebellion and your sins. If you forsake YHVH and serve foreign gods, he will turn and bring disaster on you and make an end of you: this, after he had been good to you."

But the people said to Joshua, "No! We will serve YHVH."

Then Joshua said, "You are witnesses against yourselves that you have chosen to serve YHVH."

"Yes, we are witnesses," they replied.

"Now then," said Joshua, "throw away the foreign gods that are among you and cleave with your hearts to YHVH, the God of Israel."

And the people said to Joshua, "We will serve YHVH our God and obey him."

On that day Joshua made a covenant for the people, and there at Shechem he reaffirmed for them, decrees and laws. And Joshua recorded these things in the Book of the Law of God. Then he took a large stone and set it up there under the oak near the holy place of the Lord.

See!" he said to all the people. "This stone will be a witness against us. It has heard all the words YHVH has said to us. It will be a witness against you if you are untrue to your God."

Then Joshua dismissed the people, each to their own inheritance.

Afterward, Joshua read all the words of the law--the blessings and the curses--just as it is written in the Book of the Law.

The AVIV Haggadah

There was not a word of all that Moses had commanded that Joshua did not read to the whole assembly of Israel, including the women and children, and the strangers who lived among them. Joshua 8:34

Education throughout the ages was a key part of the Torah of Moses and we read in Deut 6:20-24

In the future, when your child asks you, "What is the meaning of the decrees YHVH our God has commanded us?" Tell him: "We were slaves of Pharaoh in Egypt, but YHVH brought us out of Egypt with a mighty hand. Before our eyes YHVH sent signs and wonders—great and terrible—on Egypt and Pharaoh and his whole household. He brought us out from there to bring us in and to give us the land he promised on to our ancestors. YHVH commanded us to obey all these decrees and to fear YHVH our God, so that we might always prosper and be kept alive, as it is today. We should be careful to obey all this law before YHVH our God so that this will be our ZEDEK righteousness."

It is hoped that each year we will meet to celebrate the festivals AVIV and Sukkot remembering the unique event: the Exodus from Egypt and the harvest pilgrimages in Israel. We have visited four mountain sites- Thera, Horeb, Nebo and Gerizim/Eval and witnessed the formation of the Israelite nation as it occurred around 3,500 years ago.

Sing **VETAHER LIBENU**

Vetaher Libenu   Purify our Hearts

Vetaher libenu leavdeha bemet X2

Vetaher libenu bemitzvoteha X2

Velo nevosh velo nikalem velo nikashell

Leolam vaed

Kibeshemha THVH hagadol veha kadosh

Veha nora batachnu

Nagila nagila ve nismecha bo

Purify our hearts to worship you in truth

Purify our hearts with your commandments

We shall never be ashamed, despair or fail

For we will trust in YHVH your great, holy and awesome name

We shall rejoice and be happy with it

HAG AVIV SAMEACH

The AVIV Haggadah

The festival of Tabernacles- Sukkot was a harvest pilgrimage held in Israel at the height of the wheat and grape harvest.
All Israel was to celebrate at the chosen city for seven days and live in Sukkot for the duration of the celebration.

THE TEN WORDS AS PRESENTED IN THE MOSES SCROLL BY ROSS NICHOLS

I am Elohim your Elohim who liberated you from the land of Egypt from a house of servitude. There shall not be to you other gods. You shall not make to you, other Elohim. You shall not make for yourselves a carved thing or any formed thing that is in the heavens above or that is on the earth below or that is in the water under the earth. You shall not bow down to them and you shall not serve them. I am Elohim your Elohim.

Sanctify the seventh day. Six days I made the heavens and the earth and all that is in them and I ceased on the seventh day. Therefore you shall also cease, you and your animals and all that is yours. I am Elohim your Elohim.

Honor your father and your mother. I am Elohim your Elohim.

You shall not kill the body of your brother. I am Elohim your Elohim

You shall not commit adultery with the woman of your neighbour. I am Elohim your Elohim

You shall not steal the property of your brother. I am Elohim your Elohim

You shall not swear by my name to deceive, because I will avenge the iniquity of fathers will be upon children to the third and to the fourth generation for using my name to deceive. I am

Elohim your Elohim.

You shall not respond against your brother with a testimony of deceit. I am Elohim your Elohim.

You shall not desire your neighbour's woman, his servant, his maidservant, or anything that is his. I am Elohim your Elohim.

You shall not hate your brother in your heart. I am Elohim your Elohim.

About the Authors

The AVIV Haggadah

Chryl Elizabeth McWilliams

Chryl Elizabeth McWilliams began her career in Oklahoma with a B.A. in Theatre Arts before turning to the study of the Hebrew Bible. She is the producer of a Facebook video series on the Bible and recently wrote the first AVIV Haggadah. The Haggadah was conducted by Chryl in 2021.

Mrs. Mc Williams decided to produce an expanded Haggadah with the cooperation of Barry Page.

The AVIV Haggadah

Barry Page

Barry Page turned from the Orthodox Jewish approach some 50 years ago to devote himself to Hebrew Biblical scholarship. He focused on Hebrew linguistics, revised chronology and the theology of the book of Deuteronomy.

He has studied at Mount Scopus in Australia, the Jewish Theological Seminary in New York and Hebrew University in Jerusalem. Barry has written three books on Hebrew Biblical scholarship, the latest one being The Historical Moses Found.

www.ingramcontent.com/pod-product-compliance
Lightning Source LLC
Chambersburg PA
CBHW061317040426
42444CB00010B/2684